HAL•LEONARD

JAZZ PLAY-ALONG®

Book & Audio for Bb, Eb, C and Bass Clef Instruments

volume 102

Arranged and Produced by Mark Taylor

Jazz Pop

10 Fa...

PLAYBACK+

Speed • Pitch • Balance • Loop

To access audio, visit:
www.halleonard.com/mylibrary

Enter Code
1155-7927-4778-7085

ISBN 978-1-4234-6389-4

HAL•LEONARD®

Visit Hal Leonard Online at
www.halleonard.com

World headquarters, contact:
Hal Leonard
7777 West Bluemound Road
Milwaukee, WI 53213
Email: info@halleonard.com

In Europe, contact:
Hal Leonard Europe Limited
1 Red Place
London, W1K 6PL
Email: info@halleonardeurope.com

In Australia, contact:
Hal Leonard Australia Pty. Ltd.
4 Lentara Court
Cheltenham, Victoria, 3192 Australia
Email: info@halleonard.com.au

Visit Hal Leonard Online at **www.halleonard.com**

Explore the entire family of Hal Leonard products and resources

JAZZ POP

Volume 102

Arranged and Produced by
Mark Taylor and Jim Roberts

Featured Players:

Graham Breedlove–Trumpet
John Desalme–Saxes
Tony Nalker–Piano
Jim Roberts–Bass
Joe McCarthy–Drums

**Recorded at Bias Studios, Springfield, Virginia
Bob Dawson, Engineer**

HOW TO USE THE AUDIO:

Each song has <u>two</u> tracks:

1) Split Track/Demonstration

Woodwind, Brass, Keyboard, and **Mallet Players** can use this track as a learning tool for melody style and inflection.

Bass Players can learn and perform with this track – remove the recorded bass track by turning down the volume on the LEFT channel.

Keyboard and **Guitar Players** can learn and perform with this track – remove the recorded piano part by turning down the volume on the RIGHT channel.

2) Backing Track

Soloists or **Groups** can learn and perform with this accompaniment track with the RHYTHM SECTION only.

4

AGAINST ALL ODDS
(TAKE A LOOK AT ME NOW)
FROM AGAINST ALL ODDS

C VERSION

WORDS AND MUSIC BY
PHIL COLLINS

6

DON'T KNOW WHY

WORDS AND MUSIC BY
JESSE HARRIS

C VERSION

FIELDS OF GOLD

MUSIC AND LYRICS BY
STING

C VERSION

I SHOT THE SHERIFF

WORDS AND MUSIC BY
BOB MARLEY

IT'S TOO LATE

WORDS AND MUSIC BY CAROLE KING
AND TONI STERN

C VERSION

Killing Me Softly with His Song

WORDS BY NORMAN GIMBEL
MUSIC BY CHARLES FOX

C VERSION

ON BROADWAY

WORDS AND MUSIC BY BARRY MANN, CYNTHIA WEIL,
MIKE STOLLER AND JERRY LEIBER

C VERSION

RAINY DAYS AND MONDAYS

LYRICS BY PAUL WILLIAMS
MUSIC BY ROGER NICHOLS

C VERSION

SLOW JAZZ BALLAD

WHAT A FOOL BELIEVES

WORDS AND MUSIC BY MICHAEL MCDONALD
AND KENNY LOGGINS

C VERSION

YOU ARE SO BEAUTIFUL

WORDS AND MUSIC BY BILLY PRESTON
AND BRUCE FISHER

C VERSION

You Are So Beautiful

WORDS AND MUSIC BY BILLY PRESTON
AND BRUCE FISHER

Bb VERSION

AGAINST ALL ODDS
(TAKE A LOOK AT ME NOW)
FROM AGAINST ALL ODDS

Bb VERSION

WORDS AND MUSIC BY
PHIL COLLINS

RIT.

DON'T KNOW WHY

WORDS AND MUSIC BY
JESSE HARRIS

Bb VERSION

FIELDS OF GOLD

MUSIC AND LYRICS BY
STING

I SHOT THE SHERIFF

WORDS AND MUSIC BY
BOB MARLEY

IT'S TOO LATE

WORDS AND MUSIC BY CAROLE KING
AND TONI STERN

Bb VERSION

KILLING ME SOFTLY WITH HIS SONG

WORDS BY NORMAN GIMBEL
MUSIC BY CHARLES FOX

Bb VERSION

ON BROADWAY

WORDS AND MUSIC BY BARRY MANN, CYNTHIA WEIL,
MIKE STOLLER AND JERRY LEIBER

Bb VERSION

RAINY DAYS AND MONDAYS

LYRICS BY PAUL WILLIAMS
MUSIC BY ROGER NICHOLS

Bb Version

WHAT A FOOL BELIEVES

WORDS AND MUSIC BY MICHAEL MCDONALD
AND KENNY LOGGINS

AGAINST ALL ODDS
(TAKE A LOOK AT ME NOW)
FROM AGAINST ALL ODDS

Eb Version

WORDS AND MUSIC BY
PHIL COLLINS

DON'T KNOW WHY

WORDS AND MUSIC BY
JESSE HARRIS

Eb Version

FIELDS OF GOLD

MUSIC AND LYRICS BY
STING

Eb VERSION

I SHOT THE SHERIFF

WORDS AND MUSIC BY
BOB MARLEY

IT'S TOO LATE

WORDS AND MUSIC BY CAROLE KING
AND TONI STERN

Eb VERSION

KILLING ME SOFTLY WITH HIS SONG

WORDS BY NORMAN GIMBEL
MUSIC BY CHARLES FOX

Eb VERSION

On Broadway

WORDS AND MUSIC BY BARRY MANN, CYNTHIA WEIL,
MIKE STOLLER AND JERRY LEIBER

RAINY DAYS AND MONDAYS

LYRICS BY PAUL WILLIAMS
MUSIC BY ROGER NICHOLS

Eb VERSION

WHAT A FOOL BELIEVES

WORDS AND MUSIC BY MICHAEL MCDONALD
AND KENNY LOGGINS

YOU ARE SO BEAUTIFUL

WORDS AND MUSIC BY BILLY PRESTON
AND BRUCE FISHER

Eb VERSION

YOU ARE SO BEAUTIFUL

WORDS AND MUSIC BY BILLY PRESTON
AND BRUCE FISHER

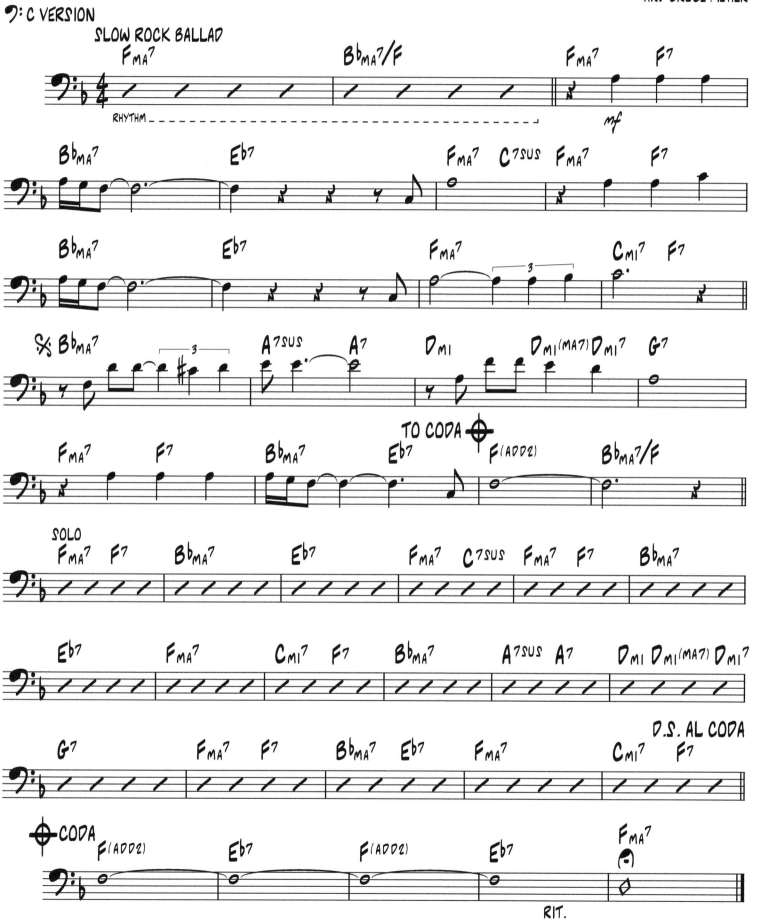

AGAINST ALL ODDS
(TAKE A LOOK AT ME NOW)
FROM AGAINST ALL ODDS

𝄢: C VERSION

WORDS AND MUSIC BY
PHIL COLLINS

DON'T KNOW WHY

WORDS AND MUSIC BY
JESSE HARRIS

FIELDS OF GOLD

MUSIC AND LYRICS BY
STING

I SHOT THE SHERIFF

WORDS AND MUSIC BY
BOB MARLEY

IT'S TOO LATE

WORDS AND MUSIC BY CAROLE KING
AND TONI STERN

𝄢: C VERSION

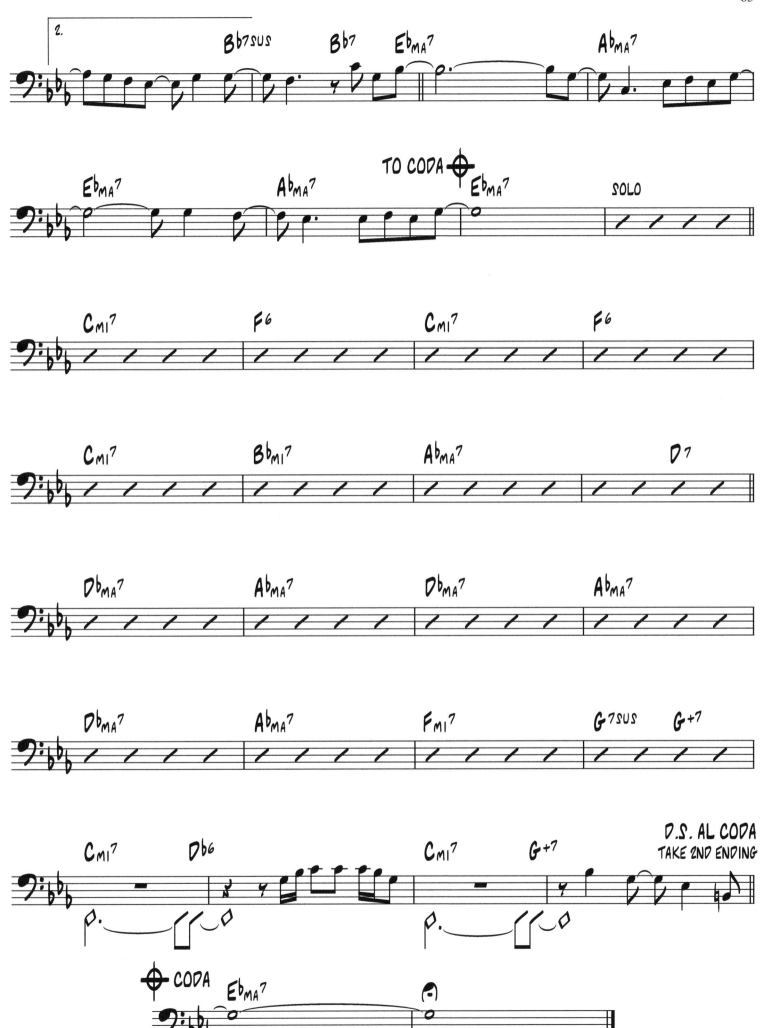

Killing Me Softly with His Song

WORDS BY NORMAN GIMBEL
MUSIC BY CHARLES FOX

𝄢 C VERSION

MEDIUM ROCK BALLAD

Eb7SUS

RHYTHM

Bbmi7   Eb7   AbMA7   DbMA7

Bbmi7   Eb7   Fmi7

Bbmi7   Eb7   AbMA7   C7

Fmi7   Bbmi7   Eb7   AbMA7

Fmi7   Bb7 /D   Eb7   DbMA7

AbMA7   Db6   GbMA7b5

FMA7   Cb7

ON BROADWAY

WORDS AND MUSIC BY BARRY MANN, CYNTHIA WEIL,
MIKE STOLLER AND JERRY LEIBER

WHAT A FOOL BELIEVES

WORDS AND MUSIC BY MICHAEL MCDONALD
AND KENNY LOGGINS

HAL•LEONARD
JAZZ PLAY-ALONG SERIES

For use with all B-flat, E-flat, Bass Clef and C instruments, the **Jazz Play-Along Series** is the ultimate learning tool for all jazz musicians. With musician-friendly lead sheets, melody cues, and other split-track choices on the included audio, these first-of-a-kind packages help you master improvisation while playing some of the greatest tunes of all time.

FOR STUDY, each tune includes a split track with: melody cue with proper style and inflection • professional rhythm tracks • choruses for soloing • removable bass part • removable piano part.

FOR PERFORMANCE, each tune also has: an additional full stereo accompaniment track (no melody) • additional choruses for soloing.

To see full descriptions of all the books in the series, visit: